Garments of the Known

Garments of the Known

Norm Sacuta

NIGHTWOOD EDITIONS

Nightwood Editions
R.R. #22, 3692 Beach Avenue
Roberts Creek, BC
Canada V0N 2W2

Printed and bound in Canada

Nightwood Editions acknowledges the financial support of the Government of Canada through the Book Publishing Industry Development Program (BPIDP) and the Canada Council for the Arts, and the Province of British Columbia through the British Columbia Arts Council, for its publishing activities.

Edited for the house by Silas White

National Library of Canada Cataloguing in Publication Data

Sacuta, Norman, 1962–
Garments of the known

Poems.
ISBN 0-88971-178-X

I. Title.
PS8587.A2384G37 2001 C11'.6 C2001-911300-5
PR9199.4.S238G37 2001

For my parents

Table of Contents

I. The South Downs Way

II. Inland

III. Night Watch

IV. Love of the Same

There is no truth, and you have set it between you;
you have been unwise enough to make a formula;
you have dressed the unknowable
in the garments of the known.

– Djuna Barnes

I. The South Downs Way

The Hills Are a Lie

Join me on this tour of the English Downs
where the Long Man is re-cut into sod,
more deeply than those pre-historic men
intended; intention the truth
easily cut into. Is this the first stencil
and so the only authority left? Forget hieroglyphs,
called down when the Rosetta Stone
turned falcons into argument.
The Long Man looks down,
a little white lying on green.

Seven horses carved on the South Downs Way.
One a gentleman thought too small
and far too hung. In 1850 he
wiped anatomy clean, made it bigger
in that big Victorian Way. He made truth.
And the story goes from there, commonly
out of the mouths of guides.
The one horse that speaks to you
and you and you.

Let's lie at night
in the hard-on at Cerne Abbas
chalk-drawn around us, those spade
made balls re-edged lovingly out of lawn,

caught between the legs of another walking
man. The fertility of you
wasted on the likes of me.

Let's lie between two rocks
and a hard place, well
on our way. *Stepping in the trepidation of flesh*
that will become myth.

Sappho, at Fifteen

for Jonathan and Dominic Harvey

I.

When Sappho dreams she runs
after what she names, Sappho.
What I keep separate she swallows
into herself. I know this only

because her paws flick like typing fingers
and her breath is short like a sprinter's.
When she wakes she knows her name
still, and cannot wonder as I do

how the South Downs in her sleep suddenly
become the pink sofa,
my bare feet once were rabbits
she was shaking, shaking in her dream.

Sappho dreams only one word:
the chalk trails that throw the moon back
brighter at itself, so white
foxes and rabbits are made shadows –

the trail, the fox, the moon, the rabbits
she shakes and shakes in her dreams
the trail the fox the moon the rabbits
she names Sappho, Sappho, Sappho.

Yet still knows this difference
as she dreams herself into things:
Sappho, Sappho, Sappho
shaking till their small necks snap.

II.

At midnight I call her by clapping
off her corner chair. She knows
this sound in old age.
Her name, still, the only word she knows –

she's made my two hands together
Sappho, Sappho
the leathery flaps of ears caressed by
her mirror image.

Yet she's taken to wandering when put out
for the final time each night,
the wide garden with twenty-four molehills
chalk-white like old dung in moonlight

is her cause, her effect.
Along the garden's edge, the rim of footpaths
she goes nose down to find her past
life without a sense of time.

I will only wait so long before slapping
barefoot up the garden steps,
to stand on the dark lawn, clapping
my most angry tone

clapping in the garden I've named in daylight
tulips, widow's breath, daffodils and rosemary,
now in darkness it could speak for itself.
I clap, afraid it might.

Applause Sappho accepts having lived so long.
And though I can't see her I know
she skips towards me, sure as a curtain call
and sees only herself clapping, clapping.

Old Story

Always behind me is your violent music
– Gwendolyn MacEwen

They are comfortable, uniform
in shirts thicker than most –
a rugby team recently victorious.
The chant is somewhat slurred
intentionally –
something they'll sharpen to pencils
surrounding a drunken woman.

Leaving the pub, I still hear
their voices, dull antiphon
with the dark ritual of these houses
above Lewes Road,
lights out, perhaps abandoned.
Built when the factories still made
England sure.

A safe distance is all
I can offer anyone, and slow
so the woman ahead feels comfort.

The empty alleys now deafening
the chant we still walk to.

My sense is less certain
these days. I'm sure my lovers speak
when their mouths are shut.
During sleep I hear machinery
beneath skin, collapsing
their brief geographies of veins.
And I'm afraid to touch them.

Afraid of the voice
I might miss on their waking.

Make no mistake: the empty alleys
merely deafen the chant.

Tower Rook

When the Ravens leave, the Tower will fall
– English legend about the
Tower of London

The clipped rook loses grasp and skitters off
the podium of imprinted brass
marking the beheadings near the Tower.
Shadow but for sound, so unlike the horrible
ravens back home: their gravelly warning across
slate roofs, before tumbling on house cats –
soft capes, suddenly sharp and clawed.

This rook has no height, will never see
the exhausted dome of St. Paul's, dull
in the afternoon sun. Its only view
an infant's, the scissor movement
of its own reach for tendons and skirts,
or a swung purse swatting it upwards
squawking to stone walls, an uneasy grasp.

Don't miss the point: the plaque
does not scratch, being made right;
it brings bright precision to history,
the names of those killed in a small
chained-off square: Anne Boleyn 1536,
Catherine Howard and Lady Jane Grey.
The grounded bird skips across the very spot,

is fed popcorn by Americans who snap
fingers back from possible harm, and laugh.
They've acquiesced, despite distant revolution,
and find excitement in the legend, accept
what is needed to maintain it. The rook
like Anne Boleyn, its injury merely
an event defining someone else's history.

And I am Canadian, odd man out as the tour
moves inside the White Tower and armoury.
Another plaque embedded beside metal suits
where the Irish triggered a bomb destroying
a tourist. The Catholicism lost
when this message was cast: merely another way
to mythologize Britain. The Tower remained standing.

Outside the rook cocks its head,
blinking at bread held out for consumption,
that dark eye more than my reflection.
It remembers altitude, a different angle –
the upturned, frightened eyes of a cat,
before casual descent. Its own event long ago,
and no one around to record it.

Nothing to Write Home About

A letter to Theresa Shea and Tim Bowling

Tonight's full moon reversed in earth-shadow;
the crescent a shutter slowly closed
until in full eclipse, it was no longer
dime-flat on cloth but a sphere slight orange,
edges dark, sloping to a hidden side.
And I was surprised by this dull fact
as when I wrote you once of a harp seal
that followed me along the coast near Wick –
a head drifted, severed on the still glass
of sea, so when it blinked and hunched forward
the slippery gulp of its length shocked me.

Blasphemy begins here: snowfall
in April that suddenly becomes rain,
and someone surprised by the recurrence.
Galileo imprisoned not for change
but for finding repetition never
the same. This past year the Pope forgave him
four centuries of indiscretion,
but in that break intended only
to keep the church holy, holy, holy.

Or the reason for this poem, the reason
always the same, always the same love lost
or gained. I'm looking at the moon now half-
covered with shadow and know I had hoped
the seal's severed head was Orpheus.
But to say so, and so in a word
make that pain clear, plain, a sphere in space
as close to me as that head had been,
bears too much repeating for one poem.

I'm alone and lonely in England.
I'm alone and lonely in England.
I'm alone and lonely in England.
And only this lament still learns.

November 22, 1963

Aldous had all bright colours in his head made brighter
the night he died. His wife injected twice on the quiet
command his hand made in hers.
                                                Do you want?
she asked and he could not say, but kept kaleidoscope
eyes open, saw the ceiling lift away in Kansas winds
that burst blue, red and violent from the edge
inward to the widening diamonds of his stare.
On the final shot his grip released,
                                                she brushed
away sweat along her slacks and wondered
what his head contained. Aldous sped
the long, slow shape a road makes – let the bullet
fall far behind his motorcade.
                                                A brave world left
with such people in it; they line parade routes
and cheer the bright, helium shapes of men.

What I Wanted to Say

O good Horatio, what a wounded name,
Things standing thus unknown, shall live behind me!
If thou didst ever hold me in thy heart,
Absent thee from felicity for a while,
And in this harsh world draw thy breath in pain,
To tell my story.

– Hamlet

The guns shoot tonight, and light your dead shape
passed hand over hand by soldiers clumsy
in their dark armour, men too young to see
how such tenderness contradicts their fates.

They carry your body as I have yearned
to know your touch without camaraderie.
You betrothed to me your womanly soul,
interpreted my blush as modesty
then, perhaps, understood my love in all
was not something you wanted to return;
through pretty Osric you made clear my role.
And now what have you damned me to recall:

The retinal shape of death in your eyes?
Your eyes! What was the colour of your eyes?

Lacuna

I am interested in seeing my eyes
only when they look at you.
– Roland Barthes

Where the blood begins. Shot
through small holes where the bone
ends, where the bone isn't, yet
there it is: what defines bone.

The day between – Saturday,
when Christ, rotting, entombed,
alone awaited resurrection – a day
of nothing watched nor proved.

Not mosquito amber, not marine fossils
high on the Rockies,
but tracks where the monster
failed to fall, limbs lifted to walk free.

The free fall through dark ocean,
bodies weighted with sodden coats,
the *Titanic*'s falling commotion
now silent around empty boots.

The perfect impressions left
where heavy bodies dissolved,
the camera's eye expects
to make contradictions resolve.

To burn to ashes
when the plane explodes,
when a fridge door latches
and the lungs implode.

For Frederick Fleet

The Titanic*'s lookout who in 1965, at the age of 76, hanged himself two weeks after his wife's death.*

There are those white objects that appear dark
and dead ahead moving closer like an illness
you're never sure you have until it's there
gliding too close, leaving
symptoms that become worse.

Did ice keep coming at you
from black-and-white dreams? Did you wake cold,
pulled from the Atlantic by your wife,
her warm hands rubbing the blood
back into your uncovered arms?

(Aboard the *Carpathia* you shaved,
 checked your chin several times that morning
 unable to accept your own skin)

And when she was gone,
taken by some cold disease –
you woke with flesh like ice and waited
smiling before you realized
help couldn't come
in time.

sing-rail trilogy

i.

ah – moon alive on rails
sing the train past houses too aware of this sound
a country too aware of rails where
trains are not for cargo too common commonly
carry people home when pubs close

sing the train passes
small stations where only once an hour they stop
and at this hour couples sway where they
try to obey the danger signs
please stand behind yellow line when trains approach

ah – shine alive on rails sing the arrival
electric contact crushes moon rock on track
the ride home down cool ridges dug a gully-made *V*
where on this warm night the moon
slips beneath wheels steel on steel
kicks out still-shining spread
flatter than a penny

ii.

square window flashes light motion
along gullies slow slanting up and away
as we move hum-rising
with electric motion

in tunnels between falmer and lewes
light-squares show motion through static
tunnel walls speed brick into lines
film past projection
our own heads steady shadows on speed

then suddenly out the carriage light leans away
where tunnel walls once were
a fox cleaning fur curving head buried
groom-motion
so used to sing-rails not even a look up
as light shoots it back into black

iii.

walk home now deep brakes beneath pavement
where long train slows motion from Victoria
the cobbled ways of lewes quiver alive
with tunnels beneath
my bare feet this warm night make
cobblestones snake-scale smooth
the graveyard road shed skin rippling
without real movement
the man behind me glory-drunk and wondering
at the slap of my arches
his own boots clump out trains that sing now two blocks away

and in the graveyard when i pull his mouth
to mine hard kissed beside
the family lost in 1967 husband wife and
three-year-old son
i'm wondering of car wrecks or passionate murder

and the sing-rails begin again
too far too many trains for him to care
notice his eyes closed my own closed too
and the rails all i hear as we kiss
my hearing of this sound trained
on trainless Canada
my eyes closed his eyes closed too   he moans

and a fox out there dark
watches us both in the singing night

II. Inland

Sonnets for the Policeman in an *Edmonton Sun* Photograph

First Photo

My cab-driver cousin ended his life
by escorting a woman to her door,
both shot by a boyfriend who saw no more
than himself in her: three ends to his life.
Taxis followed his casket, an even
processional spaced down a dark highway,
headlights on – a beauty pageant runway
to the cemetery where six strong men
would lower him, the final focused shot
by a photographer who never knew
the subject, forced the photograph into
a narrow vision, what men should be taught:
the glorious rolling of fixed white lights
reward for the escort offered that night.

Second

That same eye steals your shout, my policeman
frozen mid-stride near a child's mustang bike
handlebars folded inward, twisted like
the boy's own bent wings against the ash can:
irregular landscape beneath white sheets,
a curled hand exposed as if wrapped around
his mother's absent finger. You were found
by this telescopic lens up the street,
your mouth's private shape caught as if calling
the boy's name, a warning before his death
(or awaiting a kiss, someone's warm breath).
The photographer knows: real heroes sling
looks of unseen despair when backs are turned,
your gun at odds with the moral we've learned.

Negative

I've learned these few rules of photography:
men with tough jobs are capable of love,
escort ladies to doors and aren't above
killing women desperate to be free.
These are the two photographs that keep me
informed, in line and just outside the frame,
struggling to resist your shape, the same
image that attracts me says I can't be
a man. The photographer leaves me out,
pleases his editor, advertisers too,
for the muscled contradiction of you
maintaining the order in anguished shout.
Young men see chivalry, not what's been missed:
the dead woman's funeral, your mouth on
                                                            my lips.

Death of a Scuba Diver at West Edmonton Mall

Aura is the unique phenomenon of a distance no matter how close the object may be.

– Walter Benjamin,
"The Work of Art in the Age of
Mechanical Reproduction"

The fish need to be imagined
around him, finning
clear shadows along panes of glass.
He sees people talking where
sharks whiff their tails,
palms pressed like mimes against glass –
the walls he can see through
enclose them in a shaped cave
of air.

His own is running out.
Even if he struggles, wetsuit and tank
pinched in the filters he's come to service,
they'll wonder at the hydraulics
that make his movements so lifelike.
But no one is watching, anyway –
the sharks are real and closer.

His head tilts upward
to the bridge where shoppers
check reflections on smooth water;
their wishes flutter down to him
like tinfoil.
They imagine their coins are
the cause of occasional bubbles

that stop.

His is a better death than most –
that same day children
tumble down slides to a man-made lake,
burn under a false sun stronger than
the tilted earth provides
this northern city;
                                        everywhere
girls turn they see
themselves in mirrors and know
the thin mannequins are better dressed.
And on Bourbon Street, the bronze
hooker holds her clenched fist
forever failing to scare a cop.

The diver will be found
a day later,
and will not happen again.

Another Letter to the Dead

Monday May 5, Café La Gare, Edmonton
I wouldn't really bother, Bruce, except
your brother strolls my neighbourhood now
from a small police station beside
the Chinese incense shop.
He must wonder why
he's here at all, in a part of town
so fragrant from the shops
no one would want to steal anything.
I haven't seen him yet,
only his constable card in several cafés
taped to cash registers like a joke
about sales being final, or a personal
reminder about honesty –
I've imagined his movements as yours
when he hands over the card, wrist offhandedly
casual with the information
like a cigarette between fingers.
It's not likely, I know
he's probably more manly than that.
His uniform stiffens movement
like regulations, as he refuses
offers of incense and latte.

Saturday May 10
The bridge you jumped from can't be
seen through my campus window,
the poplars a wall along the valley
even in winter their grey branches

a dense lung filtering traffic noise.
At night, as I lock my door,
headlights blink between twigs and girders
the cars suspended as if nothing were there
that couldn't be explained.
                                        Nothing on the prairie
should ever be that high; I suppose you
wouldn't agree but it's become the city's
biggest attraction. A native girl jumped
last week and survived, mounted
the ice floe she missed and shivered,
her will restored.
She wanted to know which paramedics were single.

You wouldn't have asked, though
I know you would have wanted to. At sixteen
there are no possibilities other than
what happens in school hallways and dances.
There are no others like you. At home
your older brother's friends drop by and act
the way men are. You find them exciting
but say nothing, the distance lengthening
between what you say and feel.
                                        We both showed a healthy interest
in disaster films, the genre of our generation.
Poseidon Adventure, *The Towering Inferno*
Jaws and *Earthquake*. Did they reassure
you as they did me – liking all those deaths
made you more like other men.
To be Steve McQueen warning
no building should ever be that high,

and when you're proved right
finally getting a pat on the back
a hug from men who look
like your brother's friends.

But this is all conjecture, Bruce.
You gave me no note, no history, only
rumours around school that your parents
were left an apology.
                                        That's usually the way we leave
the world. Though you've been dead now twenty years,
the papers cover what you've missed,
the latest names and, if possible,
method of transmission, so everyone knows
what was deserved and what wasn't.

Monday May 12, Gazebo Park
Lately, I've been enjoying the possibility
of never seeing your brother. He must be
over fifty now and wondering what
you would have been like. Forgive me, Bruce,
a river leaves no trail to follow,
so I imagine his hand holding a card, casual
as a cigarette between fingers,
a bridge I don't need to see
to know it's there.

Morning after the Rodeo

Calgary, 1998

No tent is without an open invitation,
every open shirt is a pale imitation,
just what's expected, so expected
these parents newly arrived, awaiting the exodus of buggers
tell their children to stay arm's-length from those
boys who step a bit too gingerly into the morning.
These real men, real cowboys, real ones
except the children know now not to come close
just like real ones except,
flowers bloom inside those big men's jeans
when flaps flip open and boots, a bit too pointy,
point into the morning –
                                        real enough, but not really
convincing anyone.
The children keep their distance.

But it's their voices wake us
and we drown back into syrup, two-stepping, stuck,
convincing ourselves, excepting ourselves
from all these children
                                        who have been warned
Keep your distance. The distance between convincing
and a convincing cowboy. Yesterday
one stepped out of the camp shower, tossed back
the wet curtain where a half-dozen men waited
to wake up, and woke up suddenly
his immense body a chest beyond any gym and we all
thought *This is it, this is real*

but faggot-none-the-less! We were proud of
his accomplishment. He left quickly
blushing, the same embarrassment as Marilyn Monroe
seeking some acceptance of her other skills.

But who's here for that? A bull rider, sure
except we watch not the event but how it feels.
So much animal jabbing skyward one moment
his loaded jeans push down on the back, rising. Imagine
ourselves not the cowboy but between him
and the Brahma. We are ground
into nothing but him, and dream of it.

> (He knows it, too. Would not fuck anyone like us.
> Wants a mirror without what goes on in his head.
> Someone to hate what he is
> and love, watch, oh, and blow him
> while he rides.)

You see, cowboy, there is this one tragedy above all:
that love, falling hard, head-over-tail,
need not be returned to be great.

Last night a tall, thin queen with eyes
so mascara-thick they were Miss Kitty's,
crossed the dance floor in cowboy boots
fit for a concubine, a pink blouse and red wranglers –
her black hat correct except a wig
shot out its sides like Rod Stewart's.
And the panic spread too easy
cowboys two-stepped wide around her

as she wriggled to the patio,
disgust following like a snake's hiss –
exposed, exposed, hear them
Not a real cowboy
but even the Marlboro man has his toes
up around his ears, here.

Ride home to this morning.
The children keep keeping their distance and
their parents wait for the fakes to rise
so the campsite will be safe.
                                        Of a Sunday morning, ruined
by this rodeo's last, late ride.
They miss their morning paper by the campfire,
the photographs of car crashes, real captions
full of empathy.
They've cried over these
for want of fame, a need, some tragedy not too close
to befall them.
                              The world is full
of victory banquets, great big buckles
and purses almost big enough to make a living.

gay in stock's time

for Stockwell Day

i.

in alberta   we have so many words for love
they don't all fit
the page   so i change font
type the letters
so closely curling into each other
they seem to be fucking

stock writes in bold type   big
separate letters
so big he needs a billboard
   unless i stand at a distance
the single word is hard
to make out: F A M I L Y

ii.

my parents have words
for unmarried uncles   solitary men
who live alone on farms nearby
bachelor   eccentric   single
swinger   solo   career man

uncle bill dated once at sixteen
then (a great F A M I L Y mystery) never again
a brilliant skater   he loved
to check men twice his size

his job
inspecting dam sites kept him
on the road   away from his small
basement suite in calgary
he never bought a house or
felt settled in the suburbs

my father asked him to visit every christmas
a request he usually refused
to me he was absence
five white squares on the tree
signed cards with cheques
for his brother's children

my mother says he once told her
it's all right for boys to read
playboy provided they realize
it's not the way things are

iii.

religious ed olson
liked to read   too much
his neighbours all immigrants
settled near stettler many years after
he'd arrived from norway
my grandfather liked his sod-earth house
a sign he could work with his hands

but the ukrainian and german sons
(for the first time eating enough

they looked like giants beside their
stalin-era parents)   wondered at his religious books
his soft norwegian manners
                                                        evenings
they would circle the house in
dodge trucks   drink   toss large stones
against the low sloping roof
                                                        his reading
interrupted once too often
ed olson fired shots above their heads

the mounties read this event
supposed the majority right and
sent him to ponoka for tests   but doctors
pronounced him sane and he returned
a year later
the large boys with wives now
left him alone

in his seventies
he felt his legs failing
a hard blizzard outside
meant he couldn't feed the horses
ed olson placed a rifle in his mouth
and fired

the neighbours found nothing
valuable in his estate   except land
  they burned the sod house and his soft leather
books from another century
  religious lives of saints
who lived alone and had their stories
shaped celibate for uncomfortable readers
all those words for love burned dark
specks floating onto the white prairie

iv.

there are no faggots in rural alberta
in stock's time   today or yesterday
they don't fit on a page where family
is written so big
                    instead
they drive into edmonton
circle mcdougall hill in pick-ups
burnt necks   short hair
and baseball caps
  hired hands resting along
cab back windows
cupping the shoulders of pretty boys
they want
to fit into

Alberta Pick-Ups

These trucks are their lives, open and honest
as the lies they tell in Lac La Biche
to wives who've come to believe the route
back from Edmonton is an hour longer
than it is.
They are without the complication
you get with a BMW or Mercedes,
so much baggage in Vancouver's West End.
Expect a ball cap – and yes – there's one,
rim backwards a kisser, forwards means business
and don't expect anything in return.

But they often return, and do
to the parking lot below
Government Hill. Summer nights
are endless. Their truck colours
refuse to fade to grey.
Anonymity lost to passing cars, they sweat
even harder across the soft leather.

Their true fantasies are of pick-ups finally theirs,
all payments made. The others are a nuisance,
required relief for something not quite right
they've always felt, but disliked.

There've been two surprises – once, after passion,
the boy from Wapiti said
Wanna see my Hummer? And he showed me.
We barely fit the McDonald's drive-through
and drove around town sipping shakes,
everyone staring, wanting, needing
his massive truck. I felt important.
His date to the prom.

The other, a cap-forward
wanting only relief,
wore a pink rubber ring
he slid off after, and hung
on the rearview mirror
like fuzzy dice.

Summer Windigo

I saw one last summer
melt thin as heat
waves across the highway.

As I reduced speed ahead
the road crew emerged dry as bones,
shirts off in afternoon heat

(the only girl
like a traffic cop
kept cars rolling).

Resumed speed
behind me their bodies irregular
weaving like fronds in a sudden current.

New tar glistened wet
as water raced
away from me in all directions.

Warm wind through open window
whispered a solid threat:
cooler nights to come.

III. Night Watch

What of the Night?

One's life is peculiarly one's own
when one has invented it.
– Dr. Matthew O'Connor
in *Nightwood*

And what of it?
Your basement was always dark anyway,
the must of unwashed laundry
and open beams above the beds,
crosses of support, no drywall
the walls rumpled plastic of your father's
best intentions.
Those transparencies breathed
in sleep each night.

What of the night? What of it?
I thought it held nothing that darkness didn't offer,
conversation without bodies, occasional
parental questions called down stairs,
the dog panting somewhere between us
as we planned great student
election victories, who would be
the winner at year's end?

And never once, not once moving
to my bed, nowhere a hand
out of the darkness
like a fish on a midnight swim.
At thirty when I told you
I was gay too, you said

Well, what difference then
would a pass have made? It would have been the end of us.
The talk of high school as two friends parted.

And I know, I know
this is unfair, I know but
I blame you. I will always blame you.
I wish this all for you, all this and more:
not death nor the swelling
each day as days go down with blood,
but, rather the pain
that my past doesn't concern you,
and in that knowledge,
not finding what the night contains.
Knowing your best friend went out, danced,
stepped into flesh that left no mark
then came back and said
absolutely nothing.

I wish this back: the embarrassment,
what I feel when the older man I now date
walks into a bar and talks to his past.
My life is a theory, in my head.
The night is only for those who care
not to confide.

And, finally. I wish you this – my hatred.
Knowing I shouldn't but feeling the need.
That's it. Hating so completely,
and wishing you'd feel enough about me
to hate the same, just once, my friend
my dear friend.

The Lengths He'll Go

These rich guys paid six million dollars
for Secretariat after his running days
were over, since he was supposedly the
most valuable stud on the face of the
earth, and then he turned out to be a
reticent breeder, which is a fancy way of
saying homosexual. He wouldn't go near
a filly for all the sugar in Hawaii.
– Barbara Kingsolver, *The Bean Trees*

I know why you ran, your hooves
so far ahead the jockies behind
thought you were a skipping girl
with a pigtail.

It's the shape we make at a distance.

In high school I ran the union,
arranged my day with lists
so teachers would smile and grant
afternoons off class,
high marks
my ticket out of lectures.

The dull thud of bad rock music:
places my keys gave escape
when everyone else was crowded,
wanted to be crowded in
close embrace on the dance floor.

The lengths I'd go to have
an empty school
where I painted or walked halls,
the others indistinct behind
locked doors, peering after
something they'd never admit was there.

I know why you ran so fast.
The safety of lengths, eliminating comparison,
so far away no one would think
to ask any questions.

Your offspring, of course
were a disappointment.

Sleeping with Michael

Already caught in a lie.

Before the first kiss, before even
the intention of a kiss,
ten nights in Edmonton before these
two in Jasper I closed my eyes each evening
you slept on my couch
and shaped my breathing into
your arm across me.

I made you up, pacing up
the steps to where I couldn't sleep.
Desire the sounds of a house settling.

Now you're breathing beside me
the short gap between double beds
where this poem fits. You move in absence,
used to the weight of your lover beside you,
a sleep accommodating past and future.
His warmth imagined for once
without argument.

Both our dreams anticipating movement.

But your love has always been more concrete,
open-mouthed and searching
for breath on skin and a way to rest.
My own is always caught
fearful within skin, shamed into words
I'll probably never show you.

Tomorrow on the drive back
we'll see in December sun an owl,
perched solid white like a tall cone
of settled snow.
                    Its head-swivel the only
invisibility I've ever seen
come in and out of itself,
eyes too sudden towards us, green,
thoroughly without interest.

You'll drive back for photographs, the bird still
when we roll past snapping,
its head full away,
those eyes shrinking distance
we've yet to cover on the road home.

The reader left now, like me,
wondering how you'd feel in the motel dark.

For Michael, in Part

You parked, and
it was what he wouldn't do that made you
realize he only thought in parts.
(Not the complete anatomy I made of you
on our first meeting, your blue eyes and beard
burdening me with the expectation of
your entire skin.)
He wanted none of the whole
and the car enclosed you like cold lips.

So when his first fist hit
you thought only of where you weren't;
the punch an absence, like a ringing phone
unanswered, no message left so someone
would know where you were.

He kept at your face
a part you couldn't hide.
Knew your swollen mouth
would mutter fictions, and have nowhere to go.

You tell me this because
I have to stop beating myself up.
It's better to have no
such nightmares waking me. But I
fill in the blanks of my life
with dreams no less painful
just because they never happened.

Had I been there, Michael,
I would have forced his fists open
back until the fingers snapped
limp into the beautiful tendrils of sea anemones.
I would have gone back in time and stopped
his parents' coupling.
I would have kissed your eyes until
the black rings circled my lips like mascara.
I would have let you
touch any part you wanted.

In the Lottery Corp

Don't think
this is a mechanical movement,
when you poke the gambling video
and discard everything but twos-are-wild.

Sometimes the screen is so dirty from other men's hands
you have to lick your thumb so the machine can feel you.
You'd lick the screen
if you thought it would do any good.

You wanted the same thing
from your phys ed teacher,
when you were the biggest kid in class
used to illustrate wrestling moves,
his chin a sharp, slight knife
against your ribs bending you
in half to be pinned.
You wanted a hand inside his jock
his hard-on unbelievably
warm in your fist.

But that never happened.
You wouldn't take the chance.

So you draw a crowd.
Draw four deuces for 500 quarters.

Later when your money's gone,
you lie in bed and feel diamonds push through skin –
the flush you never got
and no one beside you to keep flesh down.
You briefly dream about Chance Caldwell,
press and press the thin pages of a magazine
until his thick hips feel three-dimensional
in your fist.

Back out of bed
you dress, hit the instant teller –
another sixty dollars
and only an hour before the bars shut down.

A muscular cowboy's there
and watches you touch the screen
cards you don't want flipped back,
discarded with the warm touch of your finger.

You wish you could feel something more.

Money better spent on beer,
he says, suddenly beside you
when a club flips over
and you draw a straight flush.
He stands, his hand against your back,
warm breath in your ear as he squints,
the quarters running up to one thousand
like a digital watch.
His checkered shirt is a space you want to crawl inside,

press fingers against his nipples, hair, anything with texture
except the slick surface of that screen
you're both watching.

When you cash-out he's beside you
but won't follow you home,
calls you lucky when you know you'll never be.
You almost wish he'd pound you in the alley,
his fists shattering the glass
of your eyes –
his deerskin boots blocking stars that burn
long past, before
your desire.

You'll be back tomorrow
because the money is never enough.

How to Talk to a Brushcut Man

pretend you've never touched one before
ask if you can touch it
act as if nothing's happened
use metaphors
moleskin
billiard ball
velcro
ask if you can borrow his comb
ask if he's in mourning
say nothing
say it will grow back
ask for a lock to remember him by
rub him the wrong way
comment on the nap
comment on the nape
say he looks like someone famous
elvis in *g.i. blues*
oliver north
sinead o'connor
grace jones
whisper to him and feel it
wonder how it feels moving between your legs
ask what shape he leaves on his pillow
say how much you hated the beatles
check his profession
check his politics
don't mention his ears

Down on Vegas

In casinos there is the quick
click of chips, the dollars
sound hard when they fall.

No one asks where our money's been.

Men are better organized,
give credit where it's due –
borrowers found in the desert
extended beyond their means,
their mouths dull ovals of money,
the backs of their heads gone.

Driving the interstate
you speak of astronauts, their suits so big
two men could share space.
Behind us the city shines
without the sun, retaining promise
the moon failed to.

Parked in darkness, that fear returns
of men organized – odds are
they'd make us ride naked
through the desert. The precinct's
laughter when hitting the jackpot.

Sorry boys,
luck should always be a lady.

But your warm mouth moves.
I want you
now to look up, see the rising moon
restore a silver-dollar promise
to our dark part of the desert.

For Robert – Now in College, and Finally on Stage

Isn't it grand at last to show the way
to God and not believe a word of it?
The Cocktail Party, playing Eliot's
Reilly, with his ridiculous speech on faith.

The path to God a trace of the old man's
signature; Eliot speaking secure
from his dead place: *I know the hard and sure*
route to heaven, accept the sacrifice!

But you know lies when they're spoken, Robert.
I lost you in grade seven, the day you
claimed aloud in class that holy ghosts flew
from backed-up drains in your basement to enter

your open ear. The dead spoke to you of dull
topics that made class bullies confident
in their own weak skills, their hands clenched
to fists found you cringing behind the school

and you staggered away from their laughter
those same ghosts rising with old names
from football fields – mother-of-God and male saints
promising sacrifice would make you pure.

You knew: we live life without right answers.
What is the square root of 78?
Why do grade nine boys need to hate?
Tell me what you mean by a sense of sin –

Eliot again, preaching through Reilly
weak definitions that ruin my rhyme –
but you act without belief, speak these lines
as if knowing what Eliot failed to see.

The mobs he feared, refused even to
acknowledge, are easily misled
by belief in something beyond their deaths.
They'll take his difficult route to heaven

then find the sacrifice made them merely
unhappy a long time before dying –
But you'll be on stage still, a pipe playing
children off cliffs into water nearly

shallow enough to save them.

A Fairy's Rings

I.

My neighbours cut them out like cancer,
leave margins for error, even remove
donut centres of green grass.

(An unruly mob on their lawns
battering turf. The pieces rest
like severed tails on cement.)

Still, the rings move one yard
to the next at Olympic pace.
Some gardeners won't speak

for fear of unknown transport,
no longer share mowers
hedge-clippers or green tips.

II.

Why not see what shapes
emerge? Cultivate bad designs
into Mickey or Minnie Mouse

or fill the centres with earth,
only the yellow band left like
the expanding pupil of a cat's eye

or make small cardboard arrows
for fairies to follow. Petals will
spirograph in desirable directions.

But it's dangerous to demand
circular thoughts
where lawns are perfect lines.

III.

Some moonless night they'll see me
dance small rings around blue spruce,
my movement only

measured by blocked stars.
I'll be the shadow come
to take children to the underworld.

(Their own athletic sons asleep –
straight dreams
like the hundred-metre dash)

Out of two-car ports they come, spooked
shirtless and waving spades
to batter my difference to pieces.

A Brief History of a Fundamentalist

(sonnets in reverse)

Could I understand sin more easily
if the universe were shrinking into
itself – the teacup I broke yesterday,
Doug, unshattering back up to my hand?
I've wished a hundred times you'd learn to write
your p's in *repent* properly, on benches
store windows, telephone poles and stop signs.
Why these places, anyway, for God's word?
If the universe begins contracting
again you'll watch the felt-tipped letters like
rain run uphill into the pen, the news
of world's end erasing over and over
as you walk, talk, backwards to the doomsday
message you'll have to deny authoring.

But Christian history winds down in
a forward direction, Doug, like this march –
gay men and women you pedal beside
shouting against unnatural bodies.
This is an older part of Edmonton,
trees touch here, the same sex above our signs,
green arches chapletting fags with poplar seed.
Piss off, Doug, and ponder this sign from God:
lightning on a late summer night; you count
to infinity but no thunder comes.
You move towards our event horizon
frightened when your bike wobbles too close, slows.
God's an asymptote you'll ever, never be
slowly approaching through all our black holes.

as for that cap in your back pocket

for Drew McWhinnie

it's a code   hung the right way
it tells *us* the where   and how
dependent on time of night day and
place   place is crucial

i was informed of these codes in toronto
(the ring in what ear   how hankies are tied)
by a straight friend before I was out
    whistled at on Church Street
he grimaced   began to list what to avoid
the obvious moves *we* make to signal
desire made him feel robbed   like *gay*
a word he wished he could still use

this may be the way to go
all our gestures small acts
of war   worried men moving
less and less until
they're afraid to lift a finger
statues of their own fear to be touched

so provide your straight friends
this new list

Drinking white wine.
Eating in any French restaurant.
Owning an expensive car.
Rubbing your neck in public.
Putting a wallet in your back pocket.
Attending all sporting events.
Any date with a woman who seems to be having a good time.
Wearing clothes.
Walking.

as for that cap   put it on
every action is ours
and soon the streets will be
full of only the right men
and monuments

Last night on CBC

a scientist was speaking about free will,
and the ability to build thought:
"When moving one arm
we feel the presence of the other.
And how do you teach a computer such freedom?"

Does this mean madness is nothing
more than absence, a brief inability
to remember left has right?

I'm trying to understand

your decision to sleep here
must mean you have other places to go –
like your arm now moving
up the sheet as the other slides
down under covers.

(There's lightning, look!
through the window
a morning storm off the Rockies
approaching just beyond your chest)

I'm trying to understand
understanding.

Your beard touches my hand,
your body rubs static
charges on dry sheets,
small shocks in the dark –

free will is improbable
where there's desire.

And you move again,
an approaching prairie storm
spreading out across my skin.

Hallway Light

The supple light
vinyl luggage in the hall.

Like a poor photograph,
your face has eclipsed
the light behind
and made your voice
expressionless.

Reason,
after reason you rise
and turn towards the hall,
lift the light.

Supple expressions hold
the luggage in the hall.

IV. Love of the Same

Love of the Same

I dream my mother's mausoleum.
She will have no such thing.
But I dream it, walk with footfalls
echoing before each frame,
as in a film with sound gone wrong, a song
racing ahead without the singer.

So this is my mother's mausoleum, I think
in my dream, knowing how ridiculous.
The floor is slate, pink and grey, echoing
as I approach the white stone
sarcophagus cast in her shape. I know
this dream is a memory of England –
Canterbury Cathedral's stone bishops
dead around the nave, so many
with such a long history of dying.

My mother's sarcophagus, yet I don't remember
how the mask looked – why the need?
I know her well. My dream understood.
I see only stone, smooth and white,
lifeless as memory. There is no fear in waking.
She lives still, at 73.

In life, my father struggled on a gurney
six days longer than expected. After aortic-valve
replacement he pulled at tubes catching his voice, wanted
to hear himself shout at my mother. He yanked
until nurses tied his hands to the metal catch we leaned against.

Fear grew, though he lived, pressed like
the pillow clutched against his chest – deep coughs
to clear his lungs, the pressure applied
kept his stitches from bursting.
Two years on, he can't look at the scar.

My mother wants no funeral. My father does.
This is where their opposition ends.
For in their aging they return to parents
long dead. This is no metaphor.

They have become immigrants that smile and wave
as if parting on a dock.
My father's plot – purchased beside his mother,
father, in a town that ceased to exist
when the railroad pulled out. He will rest
on the incline above Byemoor.

A second plot my mother will never use.
She has an envelope in my files
with no secrets – she will be burned to ash
and sprinkled across her mother's grave in Medicine Hat.

Our days, so many, build memory into life.
That husband and wife count their days, as days go on,
back to blood and birth and love as a child –
not love of an other. Love of the same.

Mother, Father, I am the same, but never
made your break – to make my own.
You are my lovers, as any
man with man knows. My fear grows.

And one day that dream, my mother's sarcophagus
a few steps away, the white stone
that will wake me
to a life so alone.

Exposure
(Hail Storm, July 25/77)

The canvas became green,
my parents' black outlines like
they were blocking a slide screen.
I heard them snap fasteners
to keep flaps down,
the rain suddenly hard.

The first stone made my mother stop.
Bright flashes brought spots before her
as hail made shadows
when it could.

The patterned ceiling soon heavy and cold.
She punched canvas to make stones tumble off.
My father below her moved
rapidly to mop the loose rain.

Together in one light
for a moment his lowered body,
her upheld hands,
made the shape of a deer.

Gone in darkness
the next light revealed
two separate forms.
Rain came again, turned stones liquid
racing down the trailer's side as we slept.

That morning we could see as we spoke.
The canvas hard and whole,
my father, on his back, kicked with both boots
twice before the door opened.

We emerged warm in the cold air,
saw the hail's white eyes within the ice –
the trailer steamed
like a heart cracked open.

Soft Shoe

Before Victoria Day my father walks, his body
limping chronicles of winter falls,
slow movements memories
of black ice beneath snowfalls –

as if his garden this spring weekend
might be a rug on linoleum,
the soil is tested, turned on end
to be sure the cool earth absorbs sun.

By late summer his stride
has grown to match the rows of beans,
a garden too big for his wife –
my mother watches through the backdoor screen

one foot lift, then the other
as he spreads blankets over cucumber vines.
She hopes the heavy cover
will save nothing from the coming rime.

But by autumn his gait is enormous,
heavy, sure thuds to the kitchen:
arms laden he climbs the back steps,
the sink soon full for pickling.

She stands confined to his lead:
at the counter her feet ache with a coming winter
full of memory's need –
his youth is their larder.

They'll walk the crescent before first snow,
Father three strides ahead like some scout,
Mother out of practice, summer-slow,
waiting for winter and his doubt

to rise again with each falling degree,
as the larder shelves begin to empty.

My Brother's War Models

Glued seams are meticulous,
scraped clean like the lean line separating
halves of his brain – he's kept imagination
in check with precision,
denied the artistic hemisphere
where flight first originated.

He sees angles, not the angel
who stretches fingers to touch
the face of Mary in *The Annunciation*.
He knows instead the Pieta saved
her severed nose restored
after powdery hammer blows.

He studies the cardboard cover,
real photos of Spitfires in flight
and imitates decal arrangements,
the yellow and blue targets
curling in warm water, sticking
to fingers like wet silk.

He wants them perfect
wants imitation wants conformity
just like the war.
He will not let his friends
hold them unless they
wash their hands first.

Tied with clear fishing line
they spin without crashing
gently above his bed, responding
each evening to the rhythmic currents
from his open mouth, fair weather from
a soldier born forty years too late.

My Mother's War Story

And she only thirteen then, with her older sister
on the South Saskatchewan's shore. Across the river
the captive Germans tilled dry soil into gardens.

She saw two men step dripping onto the coulee,
wipe boots as if observing rules
their mothers taught them in the Rhineland.

They asked permission first,
then sat on the blanket by her silent, wiser sister.
Jam and bread were passed.

The older man spoke elegant English
with his mouth full. The younger one nodded
shyly for ham and tea.

They took nothing more,
then left their warm, wet shapes
darkening the blanket.

Grandfather made calls.

But the prisoners were all perspiring,
their shirts soaked. The lieutenant said
all Huns look the same. Maybe one will brag.

Silly logic, really, unless he thought
something more happened
than Grandfather wanted to believe.

She doesn't see this possibility now
retelling the story, remembers only
the older man liked Marie

and that certain Germans remained,
became irrigation farmers. (Does he remember
lunch by the river the same way

she sees their heads gliding back across water?)

Radio Free

The Trans-Canada bisects Medicine Hat like this knife
coming at my Aunt Bessie in her dream. She wakes
with Bach and Mozart, her poodles, pressed
one against each side in a single bed, secure but sensing death.
Her casket passes as each dog's head rolls back
to question the hour – upside-down eyes that want her only.
She rises, the dogs plop down,
and walks the stairs to test the four front locks.

The Trans-Canada is no escape for her, only
for those who want the West Coast.
For them it is an artery. For her, an artery severed.
So many monsters pass through, who stop
make the Hat tremble, cause trouble, then run.
She has no intention of being
anywhere else. This was her parents' house
and as the dream fades, trailed by dogs, she puts
the kettle on to boil. Two a.m.
The four backdoor bolts are fine.

Tea is accompanied by a scanner
bought and tuned by a good boy, her nephew,
to pick up all the trouble. Policemen
she knew as children, troublesome but only
for raiding gardens and the apricot tree by the back porch.
They're grown now, their handsome voices, deep,
reassure her on sleepless nights
with talk of coffee shops, truck stops and an occasional
drunken native at the Assiniboia.

But this night there is no peace. The radio
shouts frantic. *McCormick's! McCormick's!*
We need back up. And as the words confirm
the worst, *shots fired,* the dogs perk up, bark
as the pop, pop, pop happens
less than a block away. What to hear first?
The radio or the air
between her and McCormick's,
where she shops for fruit and meat.
It must be the safe – she knows – the safe with a week's deposits.

This is news that will make it all the way to Edmonton.
Two robbers dead, and not a single voice lost.
But now, the air is full, silent, between her
and the store. No future imagined
with the Guyanese student who will court her
from the community college. Her doors wide open, then,
to talk of Africa, and an age difference
that will make her end his visits. No past, either,
with her father's face so pale. She goes
to wake him from a late sleep, and cannot succeed.

The sun rises. Bessie looks through the apricot tree,
listening to a quick rhythm
that will end in this same house
many years off. But the dogs must be let out
long before then, and the locks are turned
one by one by one by one.

A Poet Recalls Fiction

I have trouble with friends who want to know what happened.
And no, I'm not missing the forest for the trees –
the genus, size and shape,
even when the author cares enough,
will escape me later, become a forgotten shadow
at the edge of the moors.

I am the worst witness of another witness,
read pages and pages without memory
of a character's features.
My rhythmic eyes remember little,
move away from that tape by the door
where I should measure the criminal's height.
What difference does that make?
He robbed me, I might tell the officer.
Isn't that enough?

What's a character? It's every fear of every name
ever introduced to at parties,
crammed into *The Tenant of Windfell Hall.*
Thank god for *Anna Karenina* and *Jane Eyre.*
The title and name the same.

Let me tell you about *Jane Eyre*:

there's lightning that cleaves a tree directly in two
on the night she decides to marry. That man. The dark one
who talks roughly and has dark eyes so dark his first born
reflects back out of them. That's *Jane Eyre*.
That's all.

Don't ask me for more. I don't know
once the book is down. But open it again:
I know that point in the forest –
breadcrumbs lead home in all directions. There is no place
lost quite like it. I read pages and pages, enthralled,
then forget my way as the moon sets.

And isn't it glorious to know every word will rush at me,
like that mad woman from the attic,
when I read again tomorrow night.

Acknowledgments

Some of these poems have appeared in *Absinthe, Alberta Poetry Yearbook, The Antigonish Review, The Church-Wellesley Review, Dandelion, Grain, Matrix, New Quarterly, NeWest Review, Orbis (U.K.), Other Voices, Prairie Fire, Secrets from the Orange Couch, Torquere* and the University of Alberta Press anthology *Threshold.* "Another Letter to the Dead" appeared in *Jugular Defenses: An AIDS Anthology* (Oscars Press, U.K.). "Death of a Scuba Diver at West Edmonton Mall" and "Sappho at Fifteen" were winners of the Robin Lee Poetry Award at the University of Sussex, 1994 and 1996 respectively. The author wishes to thank the Alberta Foundation for the Arts for its financial assistance during the writing of this collection.

Special thanks to Tim Bowling for his support of my writing and input into this collection in particular, and to Theresa Shea for her friendship and long discussions about poetry and writing over the years. Thanks, also, to Bert Almon and Douglas Barbour for introducing me the art of writing poetry, and to Bonnie Bishop and Rhona McAdam, fellow poets and members of Incwell Ink. Thank you also to everyone at Nightwood Editions, and Silas White, for having faith in a first-time author.